My First Judo Book

My First Judo Book

Stephen Gadd and Tony Smith

Ippon/Crowood

First published in 1989 by
The Crowood Press
Ramsbury, Marlborough,
Wiltshire SN8 2HE

British Library Cataloguing in Publication Data

Gadd, Stephen
    My first judo book.
    I. Judo. Manuals – for children
    I. Title II. Smith, Tony
    796.8'152

ISBN 1 85223 248 X

Printed in Great Britain by The Bath Press

Contents

今日は

KONNICHI-WA

(HELLO)

7

IN THE BEGINNING

MORE THAN 100 YEARS AGO, ON AN ISLAND ON THE OTHER SIDE OF THE WORLD CALLED JAPAN, THERE LIVED A BOY WHOSE NAME WAS JIGORO KANO. HE WASN'T VERY BIG, AND SOMETIMES HE WAS PUSHED AROUND BY OTHER BIGGER AND STRONGER BOYS IN HIS SCHOOL AND IN THE STREET.

SO, WHEN HE GOT A BIT OLDER, HE THOUGHT - AND JIGORO WAS A VERY INTELLIGENT BOY:- "THERE MUST BE SOMETHING I CAN DO, EVEN THOUGH THOSE BOYS ARE BIGGER THAN ME."

NOW, NOT FAR FROM WHERE HE LIVED IN TOKYO, THE CAPITAL OF JAPAN, THERE WAS A BUILDING WITH A BIG ROOM. IT WAS CALLED A DOJO. AS HE WALKED PAST, HE COULD SEE PEOPLE THROWING EACH OTHER OVER THEIR SHOULDERS.

VERY OFTEN, HE NOTICED THAT IT WAS THE SMALLER PEOPLE WHO WERE DOING THE THROWING.

THIS WAS JU JITSU WHICH IN ENGLISH MEANS THE GENTLE ART. IT DIDN'T REALLY LOOK GENTLE TO HIM, BUT WHEN HE TRIED IT, HE FOUND THAT AFTER A WHILE HE COULD DO IT. HE WAS ABLE TO THROW BOYS QUITE A BIT OLDER AND BIGGER THAN HIM.

HE STARTED TO GO ONCE A WEEK, THEN TWICE, AND THEN THREE TIMES, AND THEN, NEARLY EVERY DAY OF THE WEEK.

HE LEARNT MANY THINGS. HE LEARNT HOW TO THROW HIS FRIENDS TO THE LEFT AND THE RIGHT, AND EVEN OVER THE TOP.

HE LEARNT HOW TO HOLD THEM ON THE GROUND SO HARD THAT ALL THEY COULD DO WAS WRIGGLE THEIR TOES.

BUT THIS JU JITSU WAS HARD AND A LITTLE DANGEROUS – AFTER ALL, JU JITSU HAD BEEN USED BY THE SAMURAI, THE WARRIORS OF JAPAN, FOR HUNDREDS OF YEARS.

HE GOT MANY BRUISES AND A FEW OF HIS FRIENDS WERE INJURED. SO AFTER A FEW YEARS, AND AFTER HE GOT HIS BLACK BELT HE DECIDED TO START HIS OWN SPORT WHICH WOULD BE MUCH SAFER, BUT STILL GREAT FUN. HE CALLED IT JUDO, WHICH MEANS THE GENTLE WAY, AND HE CALLED HIS CLUB THE KODOKAN.

THE FIRST THING HIS PUPILS HAD TO DO WAS TO LEARN HOW TO LAND SAFELY WHEN THEY WERE THROWN – EVEN WHEN THEY WERE THROWN BY A VERY TALL MAN AND WHEN THEY WERE THROWING

EACH OTHER. JIGORO KANO SAID THEY HAD TO DO IT WELL,
AND NOT HURT EACH OTHER.

HE SAID IT WAS VERY IMPORTANT TO BE POLITE.
BEFORE AND AFTER EACH PRACTICE, THE PUPILS HAD
TO BOW TO EACH OTHER.

JUDO BECAME VERY
POPULAR VERY QUICKLY. FIRST
OF ALL, IT WAS POPULAR IN JAPAN.
BUT JIGORO, WHO WAS CALLED
SENSEI (IT MEANS TEACHER
IN JAPANESE) TRAVELLED
RIGHT ACROSS THE WORLD
TO TEACH PEOPLE HIS JUDO.

HE DIDN'T ONLY TEACH
ADULTS BUT BOYS AND GIRLS AS WELL. SO NOT ONLY
DID ENGLISH CHILDREN, FRENCH CHILDREN AND
AMERICAN CHILDREN LEARN THIS NEW SPORT, BUT
THEY EVEN LEARNT SOME JAPANESE WORDS: THE
NAMES OF JAPANESE THROWS AND HOLDS.

FOR EXAMPLE, THEY CALLED THE BODY DROP THROW
'TAI-OTOSHI' AND THE SCARF HOLD 'KESA GATAME.'

IN 1964, JUDO WAS SEEN IN THE OLYMPIC GAMES
FOR THE FIRST TIME, AND NOW IT IS ONE OF THE MOST
POPULAR SPORTS IN THE OLYMPIC GAMES.

AND ALL BECAUSE ONE SMALL BOY IN JAPAN
WAS PUSHED AROUND BY BULLIES.

HOW TO DRESS

YOUR JUDO SUIT IS CALLED JUDOGI. IT HAS A JACKET, TROUSERS AND THE BELT. WRAP THE BELT AROUND YOUR WAIST. TIE IT IN A NEAT REEF KNOT AT THE FRONT.

BELT TYING

REMEMBER:
ALWAYS KEEP YOUR JUDOGI CLEAN.

受身

UKEMI

'UKEMI' MEANS BREAKFALL. WITH A GOOD BREAKFALL, LANDING IS EASY.

SLAP THE GROUND WITH YOUR ARM JUST BEFORE YOU LAND... AND THE LANDING WON'T HURT.

KEEP YOUR HAND
OPEN WHEN YOU SLAP
THE GROUND... AND YOUR
HAND WON'T HURT.

ROLLING BREAKFALLS

IMAGINE...YOUR ARM DRAWS A CIRCLE RIGHT THROUGH YOUR LEGS.

YOUR BODY FOLLOWS IT AND YOU ROLL OVER LIKE A BALL.

WHEN YOU GET REALLY GOOD
AT ROLLING BREAKFALLS, YOU
WON'T GET HURT EVEN IF YOU
TRIP UP PLAYING FOOTBALL ON
A HARD PLAYGROUND.

TORI AND UKE

TORI IS THE ONE WHO IS DOING THE THROW
UKE IS THE ONE WHO IS GOING OVER... SPLAT.
A GOOD TORI THROWS HIS UKE WITH A CLEAN
AND SAFE THROW. A GOOD UKE GOES WITH THE
ACTION, AND DOES A GOOD BREAKFALL.
ALL WORLD CHAMPIONS CAN DO BOTH.

TACHI-WAZA

(STANDING TECHNIQUES)

THE MAIN AIM IN JUDO IS TO THROW YOUR PARTNER IN THE AIR AND LAND HIM FLAT ON HIS BACK. THIS GIVES YOU THE PERFECT JUDO SCORE OF IPPON. THERE ARE MANY WAYS OF DOING THIS USING YOUR HANDS, YOUR BODY AND YOUR FEET. EACH ONE HAS A JAPANESE AND AN ENGLISH NAME. BEFORE VERY LONG, YOU WILL BE ABLE TO THROW WITH TAI-OTOSHI, O-UCHI-GARI, O-SOTO-GARI, TSURI-KOMI-GOSHI AND MANY OTHERS TOO. PRACTICE MAKES PERFECT, BUT ONLY IF YOU PRACTISE THE RIGHT THING!

崩し

KUZUSHI

(BREAKING THE BALANCE)

IF UKE IS WOBBLING OFF-BALANCE, HE IS EASY TO THROW.

IF HE IS STEADY AND WELL-BALANCED, HE IS MORE DIFFICULT TO THROW.

THE FIRST JOB IS TO GET UKE OFF-BALANCE.

IN JUDO, THERE ARE EIGHT POINTS OF BALANCE. YOU MUST CHOOSE THE RIGHT POINT OF BALANCE FOR THE RIGHT THROW.

MAKE A MISTAKE AND NOTHING WILL HAPPEN — OR YOU WILL BOTH COLLAPSE ON THE MAT IN A HEAP.

TIMING

IN JUDO YOU HAVE TO ATTACK AT THE RIGHT TIME. IF YOU DON'T YOU MISS THE BUS. YOU'VE GOT TO BE IN THE RIGHT PLACE AT THE RIGHT TIME — SO GET IN STEP!

STANDING REI

(STANDING BOW)

IN JAPAN, PEOPLE DON'T SHAKE HANDS
WHEN THEY MEET. THEY BOW TO EACH OTHER.
JUDO CAME FROM JAPAN, SO BEFORE EACH
PRACTICE, WE BOW TO EACH OTHER AND
AFTER EACH PRACTICE, AS A WAY OF SAYING
THANK YOU, WE BOW TO EACH OTHER AGAIN.
IN ONE JUDO CLASS, YOU DO A LOT OF BOWS.

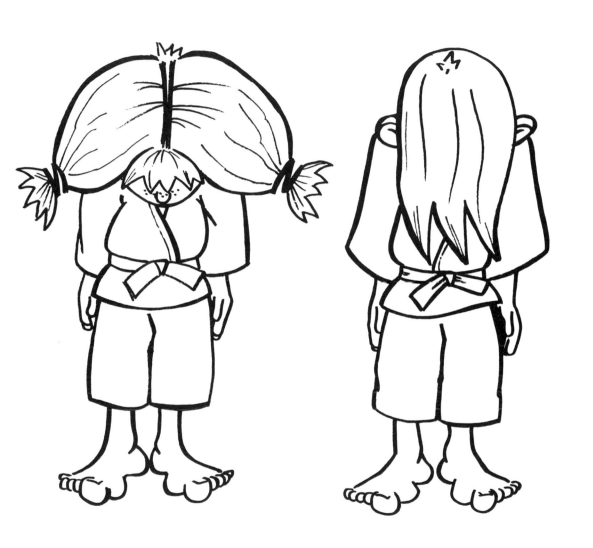

体落

TAI-OTOSHI

(BODY DROP)

1

THIS IS A VERY USEFUL THROW FOR EVERYONE - LITTLE PEOPLE OR BIG PEOPLE. YOUR HANDS PLAY A VERY IMPORTANT PART. TAKE A STRONG GRIP ON UKE'S SLEEVE AND A STRONG GRIP ON UKE'S LAPEL, PULL ON BOTH TO TIP HIM OFF BALANCE.

2 (AFTER TURN-IN)
PULL THE SLEEVE GRIP AROUND.
PUNCH THE
LAPEL GRIP
ACROSS.

3 BUT REMEMBER—
PUNCH THE JACKET NOT UKE.
IF YOU PUNCH YOUR PARTNER IN JUDO
YOU'LL GET LOADS OF
PENALTIES.

釣込腰

TSURI-KOMI GOSHI

(DRAWING HIP THROW)

1 THIS THROW MAY FEEL AWKWARD AT FIRST, BUT IT GETS EASIER. PUSH THE LAPEL GRIP UP TO THE SKY SO THAT UKE COMES UP ON TO HIS TOES.

2 THEN AIM IT OVER YOUR HEAD.

3 ONCE UKE IS IN THE AIR, A SMOOTH PULL WITH THE SLEEVE GRIP WILL PUT HIM ON HIS BACK.

大タト刈

O-SOTO-GARI

(MAJOR OUTER REAP)

1 PULL UKE'S WEIGHT ONTO THE LEG YOU ARE ATTACKING.

2 NOW CHOP AWAY HER LEG. MAKE SURE YOU KEEP YOUR TOES POINTING DOWNWARDS.

3 DON'T LET GO, BUT CONTROL UKE ALL THE WAY DOWN TO THE MAT.

大内刈

O-UCHI-GARI

(MAJOR INNER REAP)

1 PIN ALL UKE'S WEIGHT ONTO HER LEADING LEG. IMAGINE YOU ARE DRAWING A CIRCLE ON THE MAT WITH YOUR BIG TOE.

2

KEEP YOUR BIG TOE ON THE MAT UNTIL UKE IS ON HER BACK.

3

NOW HOOK IT!

小内刈

KO-UCHI-GARI

(MINOR INNER REAP)

1 THIS THROW SENDS UKE BACKWARDS.
SWEEP UKE'S FOOT AWAY JUST BEFORE IT HITS THE MAT.

2 KEEP ON SWEEPING UNTIL UKE HAS LANDED ON THE MAT—SEE IF UKE CAN DO THE SPLITS!

3 PUSH THEM ALL THE WAY DOWN TO THE MAT.

大 腰

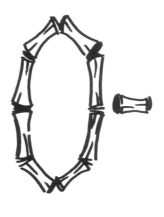

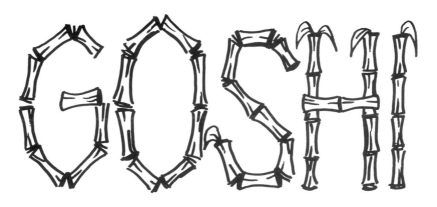

(MAJOR HIP THROW)

1

WHEN YOUR ARM IS WRAPPED AROUND UKE'S WAIST, PULL HIM IN.

2 DON'T FORGET TO BEND YOUR LEGS.

3 VERY STRONG PULL WITH THE SLEEVE GRIP TO DRAW UKE OVER YOUR HIP.

一本背負投

IPPON-
SEOI-NAGE

(ONE ARM SHOULDER THROW)

1 LOCK YOUR ARM INTO UKE'S ARMPIT, STEP IN QUICKLY, KEEPING A STRAIGHT BACK...

2 BUT WITH YOUR LEGS BENT AND SPRINGY. NOW UKE SHOULD BECOME AIRBORNE.

3 PULL HARD ON THE SLEEVE GRIP TO PUT UKE ONTO HER BACK.

巴 投

TOMOE-NAGE

(STOMACH THROW)

1 THIS IS AN ADVANCED THROW. IT IS SHOWN WITH A LEFT HAND GRIP. THE LEFT HAND TAKES THE COLLAR AND THE RIGHT HAND TAKES THE SLEEVE. WHEN YOU START TO LEARN IT, JUST ASK UKE TO DO A FORWARD ROLL OVER THE TOP. ALWAYS START WITH A STEP FORWARD.

2 THEN TUCK
INTO A BALL
AND FALL
GENTLY ONTO
YOUR BACK.

3 AS UKE ROLLS OVER YOU,
STRAIGHTEN
YOUR LEG.
BOINNNG!
OVER THEY GOOOOO!

IF YOU DON'T THROW YOUR PARTNER PERFECTLY, YOU HAVE A CHANCE TO FINISH HIM OFF ON THE GROUND.

寝技

NEWAZA

(GROUND WORK TECHNIQUES)

押込技

OSAE-KOMI WAZA

(HOLDS)

IF YOU GET YOUR WEIGHT AND BALANCE RIGHT,
EVEN A MOUSE CAN HOLD DOWN THE BIGGEST BOY
IN THE SCHOOL.

HOW TO SCORE WITH NENAZA.

YOU HAVE TO HOLD YOUR PARTNER FLAT ON HIS BACK FOR 30 SECONDS. THIS GIVES YOU THE 10 POINT SCORE OF IPPON AND THE CONTEST STOPS IMMEDIATELY. BUT... IF HE ESCAPES BETWEEN 25 AND 29 SECONDS, YOU ONLY GET 7 POINTS, A WAZA-ARI. THEN YOU HAVE TO START ALL OVER AGAIN.

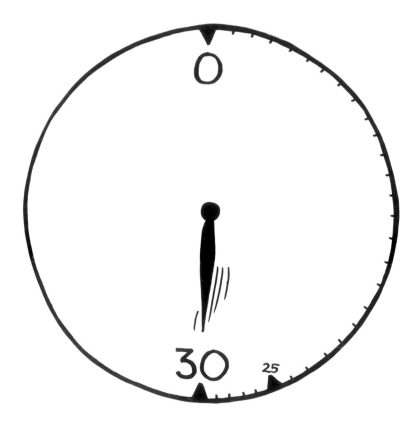

IPPON!!

KNEELING

REI

(KNEELING BOW)

KESA-GATAME

(SCARF HOLD)

KEEP UKE'S ARM TUCKED TIGHT UNDER YOUR ARMPIT. KEEP YOUR HEAD DOWN. SPREAD YOUR LEGS WIDE FOR SAFE BALANCE.

1

2

CHECK THE POWER POINTS!

横四方固

YOKO-SHIHO GATAME

(SIDE FOREQUARTERS HOLD)

PULL UKE TIGHT INTO YOU. IMAGINE YOU ARE
PINNING HIM TO THE GROUND. DIG YOUR HIPS INTO
THE GROUND.

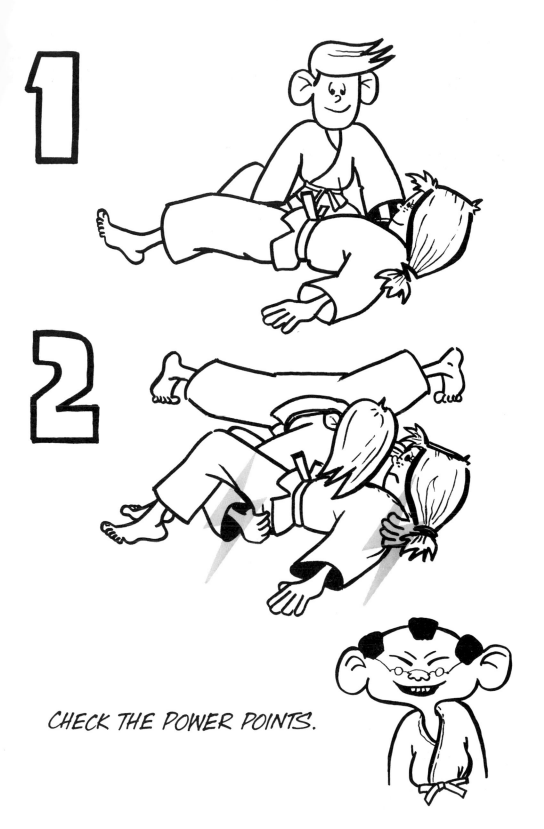

CHECK THE POWER POINTS.

上四方固

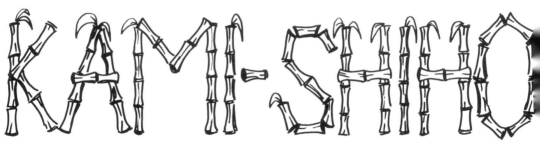

KAMI-SHIHO GATAME

(UPPER FOREQUARTERS HOLD)
KEEP YOUR HEAD FLAT ON UKE'S CHEST. TRAP
BOTH OF UKE'S ARMS INSIDE YOUR ARMS. HOLD
ONTO UKE'S BELT WITH BOTH HANDS. TIGHT HANDS
BUT SPRINGY LEGS.

ARE YOU PLUGGED INTO
THE POWER POINTS?

縦 四 方
固

TATE-SHIHO GATAME

(UPRIGHT FOREQUARTERS HOLD)
TUCK YOUR LEGS UNDER UKE'S BACK OR LEGS.
DON'T GRAPEVINE YOUR LEGS AROUND UKE'S
LEGS BECAUSE THIS COULD BE DANGEROUS.
YOU COULD GET A PENALTY (NOT A FREE KICK!).

IF UKE BOUNCES AROUND UNDERNEATH, HOLD ON TIGHT AND RIDE HIM LIKE A WILD HORSE!

後袈裟固

USHIRO-KESA-GATAME

(REVERSE SCARF HOLD)

IT'S JUST LIKE A BACK-TO-FRONT KESA-GATAME,
BUT REMEMBER, ONE HAND HOLDS UKE'S BELT.
WHEN EVERYTHING IS TIGHT, YOU CAN SIT BACK
AND ADMIRE THE VIEW.

DON'T BLOW A FUSE—
BUT CHECK THE POWER
POINTS.

JUDO EXERCISES

LEAP-FROG

CAT DIPS

STAR
JUMPS

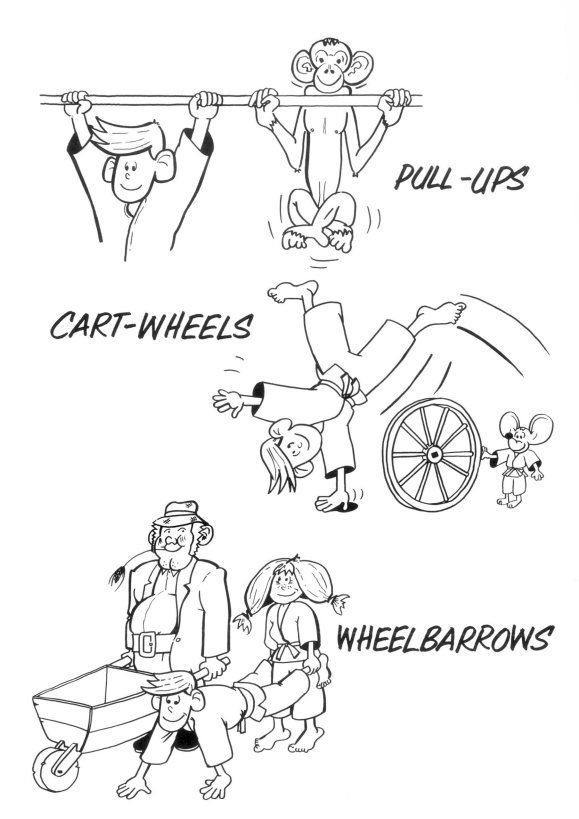

PULL-UPS

CART-WHEELS

WHEELBARROWS

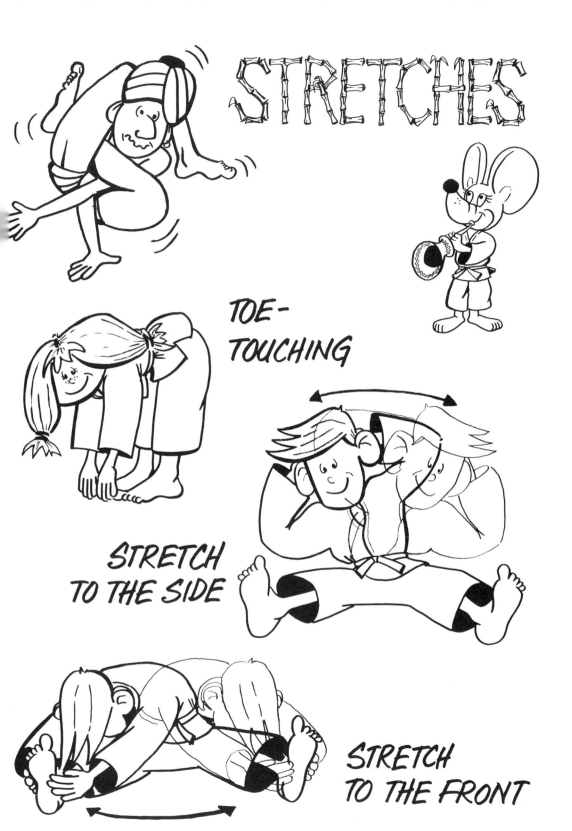

STRETCHES

TOE-TOUCHING

STRETCH TO THE SIDE

STRETCH TO THE FRONT

さようなら

SAYONARA

(GOODBYE)